Animal Offspring

Gorillas and Their Infants

by Margaret Hall

Consulting Editor: Gail Saunders-Smith, Ph.D.

Consultant: Jane T. Dewar, Founder
Gorilla Haven, Morganton, Georgia

Capstone press

Mankato, Minnesota

Pebble Plus is published by Capstone Press
151 Good Counsel Drive, P.O. Box 669, Mankato, Minnesota 56002
http://www.capstone-press.com

1 2 3 4 5 6 08 07 06 05 04 03

Library of Congress Cataloging-in-Publication Data
Hall, Margaret, 1947–
Gorillas and their infants/by Margaret Hall.
v. cm.—(Pebble plus: Animal offspring)
Includes bibliographical references (p. 23) and index.
Contents: Gorillas—The infant—Growing up—Watch gorillas grow.
ISBN 0-7368-2108-2 (hardcover)
ISBN 0-7368-4645-X (paperback)
1. Gorilla—Infancy—Juvenile literature. 2. Parental behavior in animals—Juvenile literature. [1. Gorilla. 2. Animals—Infancy.] I. Title.
QL737.P96 H357 2004
599.884'139—dc21
2002155606

Editorial Credits
Sarah L. Schuette, editor; Kia Adams, series designer; Jennifer Schonborn, cover production designer;
    Kelly Garvin, photo researcher; Eric Kudalis, product planning editor

Photo Credits
Bruce Coleman, Inc./Michael Wickes, 20 (left)
Corbis/Tim Davis, 9; Tom Brakefield, 15
Creatas, cover
James P. Rowan, 10–11
Minden Pictures/Konrad Wothe, 1, 13; Gerry Ellis, 4–5, 17, 21 (left); Frans Lanting, 7, 21 (right)
Visuals Unlimited/Bill Kamin, 19; Gary Randall, 20 (right)

Note to Parents and Teachers

The Animal Offspring series supports national science standards related to life science. This book describes and illustrates gorillas and their infants. The images support early readers in understanding the text. The repetition of words and phrases helps early readers learn new words. This book also introduces early readers to subject-specific vocabulary words, which are defined in the Glossary section. Early readers may need assistance to read some words and to use the Table of Contents, Glossary, Read More, Internet Sites, and Index/Word List sections of the book.

Word Count: 98
Early-Intervention Level: 12

Table of Contents

Gorillas

Gorillas are strong mammals.
Young gorillas are called
infants. Gorillas and
their infants live in Africa.

Gorillas live in family groups called troops. A male gorilla is a silverback. A silverback mates with a female gorilla.

The Infant

A female gorilla usually gives birth to one infant.

Infants drink milk from
their mothers.

Infants sometimes ride on
the backs of their mothers.

Growing Up

Infants grow and become young gorillas. Young gorillas play and climb.

Young gorillas learn
to find food. Gorillas
eat plants and bark.

Young gorillas leave
the troop after about
eight years. Then they
live with a new troop.

Watch Gorillas Grow

birth

adult after about 10 years

21

Glossary

Africa—one of the seven continents of the world

infant—a very young animal; a gorilla infant depends on its mother for 3 to 5 years.

mammal—a warm-blooded animal that has a backbone; mammals have hair or fur and feed milk to their young; gorillas have thick hair.

mate—to join together to produce young

silverback—an adult male gorilla; silverbacks have gray or silver hair on their backs.

troop—a group of animals that lives or moves together; a troop works together to teach young gorillas how to live and find food.

Read More

Diamond, Claudia C. *Gorilla Families.* The Rosen Publishing Group's Reading Room Collection. New York: Rosen, 2002.

Frost, Helen. *Gorillas.* Rain Forest Animals. Mankato, Minn.: Pebble Books, 2002.

Johnston, Marianne. *Gorillas and Their Babies.* A Zoo Life Book. New York: PowerKids Press, 1999.

Milton, Joyce. *Gorillas: Gentle Giants of the Forest.* Step Into Reading. New York: Random House, 2003.

Internet Sites

Do you want to find out more about gorillas and their infants? Let FactHound, our fact-finding hound dog, do the research for you.

Here's how:

1) Visit *http://www.facthound.com*

2) Type in the **Book ID** number: **0736821082**

3) Click on **FETCH IT.**

FactHound will fetch Internet sites picked by our editors just for you!

Index/Word List